Poetic Witticisms-
A Series of Thoughts Composed as Poetry

Luke Mayo

BookLeaf Publishing
India | USA | UK

Presentation by *BookLeaf Publishing*

Web: www.bookleafpub.com

E-mail: info@bookleafpub.com

ISBN: 9789358736458

First edition 2023

This book is dedicated to its readers. Whatever you have to contribute to the world, may you find the courage to do it.

ACKNOWLEDGEMENT

So many people have contributed to my life, all of whom are owed a debt of gratitude by me.

My university colleagues and lecturers have helped me to find my creative voice. Also my charity coworkers have enabled me to find the life experiences on which my poetry is based.

Most of all, my family, for standing with me and guiding me on my life's journey, and without whom my poetry endeavours would be literally impossible to achieve.

Big, warm thanks to you all.

PREFACE

Every person has something they contribute to the world. It could be a book, a painting, a song, a sculpture, a scientific thesis, a business or anything.

Whatever it is, our responsibility and our duty is to share our contribution with the world. People may not like it or understand it, but it's a disservice to ourselves not to put our contribution into the world.

This book is one of my contributions. As a lover of words and poetry, I feel like it's a worthy effort to put this out there.

Please read and enjoy.

PREFACE

Every person has something they contribute to the world. It could be a book, a painting, a song, a sculpture, a scientific thesis, a business or anything.

Whatever it is, our responsibility and our duty is to share our contribution with the world. People may not like it or understand it, but it's a disservice to ourselves not to put our contribution into the world.

This book is one of my contributions. As a lover of words and poetry, I feel like it's a worthy effort to put this out there.

Please read and enjoy.

Chilling with the Graves

Sticks and stones may break my bones
In the graveyard I'm surrounded by them

I pass by here on my daily walks
Sometimes I pause for a moment
Soak up the vibes

The dead park their bodies here
Their souls move on to new things
Their tombstones recount their existence

Sometimes I wonder
Do they know I'm here?
Are they here with me?
What kind of people are they?
Would we be friends?

All I know is this
I'll join them one day
As are we all

I may as well get to know them now
We'll be spending plenty of time together

Whatever follows death

Afterlife
Oblivion
We'll be there together

What Nobody Sees

What you did to me killed my will to live
I now need a help that none can give
The pain burns inside for year after year
My soul screams alone where none can hear

Your deeds haunt my face and behind my eyes
Though you hide what you did with deceit and
lies
You boxed me in deep and you gave me no
choice
Though you didn't expect me to find my voice

The screams of my soul at last become known
My words shared with people will not be alone
The damage you caused cannot be undone
Though you who once chased me must now turn
and run

I've taken the chance to grow and mature
So results of your actions come back to your
door
All bad deeds have consequences, that much is
true
And I'm here to make sure this applies to you

Shelter in Sensory Storms

Bright lights and big noises outside me
A soul frozen in fear inside me
Too much information to download
No space nor time to complete the process

Eardrums exploding
Eyes fading out
Brain spiralling

Alone I'm intoxicated by a sensory overload
With you I'm calm
For you are my safe space

You protect me from danger
You soothe my endless doubts
You settle my thundering brain
You help me do what I need to do

The world will always be sensory
You help me to manage the overload

For recognising
For acknowledging
For caring
For loving

For saving

Thank you so much

Diagnosis and Me

The doctor told you who you are
You were given a piece of paper
A word you need to live with

Your diagnosis

I have a diagnosis too
I carry it with me just like you
We were given different things
The fact that we were given them unites us

We are on different journeys
Facing different foes
But we can face them together

The monsters try to isolate us
We need not accept it
The monsters lie to us
We can choose not to engage

You are you
I am me
We can be us

We can defeat our demons together
If we so choose it

A Face Without Feeling

Joy dances within me
My face doesn't register
Rage explodes like a supernova
My face doesn't register
Sorrow drowns my soul
My face doesn't register

Carved in a frown
Set in a furrow
Permanently peeved
This is what I look like

No emotion can stir it
No reaction can sway it
My face stays stock still

Though a volcano erupts within me
Swirling and blasting
None of it will show
My face keeps it like a secret
Disguising the emotional outpouring

My heart clamours for expression
My face settles for acceptance

It is what it is

Words Not Done

"I will do this"
"I'll make the change"
"I'll stop it"
"I promise"

Endless statements
Weeks and months
"I promise" didn't happen
We're still here
You're still doing and not doing

"I didn't mean to do it"
"Please don't be angry"
"I'm really sorry"

Why is this your third apology?
Actions repeated
Misdeeds are an unstoppable force
"Sorry" is added on the end
The wheel turns again
It never stops

Those words you say
You don't mean them

Why make the effort to speak?
Why waste your breath?
Why don't you just do what you do?
Why do you preach the opposite?

Words and actions
Moving against each other
Clash of the titans

This isn't how it should be

Those who are Cancelled

Life's non-subscribers
They don't immediately agree
They ignore the screaming mob of conformity
They resist the calls to blend with the norm

Cancelled is the new gallows
You're not stoned or shot now
You're treated like you don't exist

If only baying crowds realised
After they've had their way with you
 Long beyond their abandonment
You're still here
Years ahead to be fulfilled
But no life to live
Because they took it away

Cancelled people
So easily forgotten
Not so easy to actually stop them
They're still going
Still a story to be told

How will history remember the cancelled?
How will it recall those who did the cancelling?

Our treatment of each other
The consequences of our righteousness
Ripples in the water
Leading where?
The future holds the answers

Good luck

Choice of Poison

Give us this day our daily poisons
They keep our lives going
They ruin our lives

Drugs and alcohol
Internal and external
Altering perceptions
Life's traumas drained of their edges
Makes the pain less immediate
Forces the death to be more immediate

Physical interludes of sex
Joys of contact
Sensory pleasures
Distracting from problems
Deprives of fulfilment

Life's endless dramas
Disaster after disaster
No space in between
So much to complain about
Life feels incomplete without them
Life is joyless with them

The things that destroy us

We seek them out
We are drawn to them
Moths to a flame
Prey to a predator

Humans are architects of their destruction

Doormat Syndrome

"I can't do it"
"I need help"
"I'm not available"

Words like a foreign language
I was unable to speak them
Even when I did
Ignored
Dismissed
Overruled

Endless demands
Stretched to fit them all
No boundary was uncrossed
No limit untraversed
I was taken to depths of despair
All because I allowed myself to be

No more

Marking a boundary
Like the astronaut's moon flag
People were shocked
Protests were screamed
The sky erupted with rebellion

The flag of my boundary stayed
The people who used me didn't
Because I dared to say no

Those who trampled my doormat
They dare not go near me now
Because they know I'm not who I was
I claim independence
I claim free will
I claim my own personhood

I am better

The Speed of Judgement

The streets we wander
The people we pass
This guy's a wrong 'un
That one's a loser

Histories hidden behind beards
Stories residing within faces
One glance and we know them all

Except we don't

The things we see
Why do we think it's the whole story?
No whole story is on display
Yet we assume it is
Assumptions kill relationships
All because we refuse to learn

The homeless guy we thought was a criminal
Turns out he was screwed by his employer
The single mum with a rabble of kids
Abandoned by her only love

The people we don't see as people
They're still people

Our judgement changes nothing
No extra points for doing it quickly
Speed makes it no more accurate
We may still be wrong

Keep your judgement to yourself

Faith Goes Tumbling

Public legends
Earners of respect
Workers towards good causes
Purveyors of talent
Life is full of them

Emerging from the sewers
Cringing in the daylight
Dirty secrets
Bigoted comments
Vile misdeeds

Just like that
Respect is gone
Years to gain
Seconds to lose

The faith we once had
Squandered and taken for granted
We loved you
We praised you
We admired you
We raised the flag for you

Not any more

Farewell faith
Goodbye heroism
Welcome ignominy
Onward to an empty future

The path trodden by many
Don't be the next on this road of tumbling faith

Things We Can't See

What do you think?
What are your interests?
What keeps you going?

People get so angry
So passionate
So riled
Conspiracies about the government
Myths and legends which encapsulate the mind
No proof but certainty is real

You know what else is real?
The world around you
The problems surrounding you
The life you're living
You could be amazing
But you're fixated on the abstract
Things you can't control

A million likes
A billion friends
Not friends but strangers
Never met before
Except through a screen

"Thank you for joining this new social media"

A massive audience of people you've never met
It's given priority over your nearest and dearest
The people close to you who love you
Ignored and relegated aside
All to get a thumbs up from the unknown and
unseen

Our lives are lived for what we can't see
The things we do see
What if we lived for them?

Victim Worship

A world of history
Rich in suffering
The human race
Defined by ongoing pain

Languishing in poverty
Undernourished bodies
Slaughtered by war
Decimated by disease
Ravaged by crime

How far we have come
Humans on the rise
As the problems rise
So does our will to overcome
Facing strife with strength
We are unstoppable

At least some of us are

For so many of us
Suffering became such a norm
We know nothing else

Victim of circumstances

Victim of the world
Victim of other people
Victim of our own mind

Generated by trauma
Feeding off pity
That's what the victim worshippers do

No problems in life?
They'll create one

Humans will always be victims
Some of them by choice

Mangled Memories

The stories we've lived
We've seen wonders and horrors
Performed miracles and terrors
Experienced blessings and torments

Or did we?

Cast your mind back
What do you see?
Blankness
Emptiness
Nothing

The images that hove into view
Do they resemble reality?

Are you sure?

We can never really know
Our own perception is valid
But it's never perfect
The world is bigger than us
Reality is more complex than our small minds

Memories are memories

Facts are facts
Not all may correlate
This is something we should remember

Misdeeds From History

The people we see
They go about their lives
Keeping on keeping on

How little we know
What lies behind them
What's been seen
What's been done
What they never want discovering

Bullying here
Assaulting there
Victims' lives ruined
Left in the dust
The one that did it moves on
Through space and time

It's been years
Decades
They've been sitting on it like a hen on an egg
Guarding it like a dragon's treasures
Fending off those who wander near

Illusions
Verbal tricks

Gaslights galore
Tricks of the trade
They keep the misdeeds safe from discovery

What's being hidden?
One can only wonder

Artificial Revolution

Soulful art by technology
Voices recreated by singers long gone
The economy left to the fate of the man-made

Artificial Intelligence is here

The more it does
The less we do

Our jobs are done
Our hobbies are complete
Our deceased are still with us

Where does it end?

Click of a button
No effort needed
AI power increases
Human worthiness decreases

Human are still here
But our lives are empty
The things we do
The things we love
Taken away

Subverted of value

AI's place in society
This is it

Body Acceptance

Marginalised people
Those shunted to one side
They claim their place in society

LGBTQ
Disabilities
Religions
And one more

The overweight

Some have no choice
They are what they are
They try to manage their body
Their body has other ideas

Their respect in society is deserved

What see you getting bigger?
The excuses
The laziness
The unthinking demands for accommodation
The refusal to consider anything else

Then the problems emerge

Organs fail
Limbs wither
Lives end
But still respect must come forth
Even when they choose to allow their body to
fall to ruin

Contributing to society
Doing good things to earn respect
It's easier when your body doesn't murder you

Body acceptance is important
So is caring for your health

Unreal Reality

The things we thought we knew
Disappearing one by one

Males and females
None of us are allowed to be either one
Our identities are invalid
Our bodies mean nothing

The passing of time
Measuring the day
What we do and when
We're told it's a scam
Twenty-four hours in a day
Not any more
Hours and days are meaningless

The world around us
Our sights
Our sounds
Our sense
Our surroundings
Simulated and unreal
How and by whom?
Unknown

What once was reality
It's no longer real
Everything is in flux
Stability is gone

I miss it